CHINA
the people

Bobbie Kalman

The Lands, Peoples, and Cultures Series

Crabtree Publishing Company

The Lands, Peoples, and Cultures Series
Created by Bobbie Kalman

Writing team
Bobbie Kalman
Christine Arthurs

Editor-in-Chief
Bobbie Kalman

Editors
Janine Schaub
Christine Arthurs
Margaret Hoogeveen

Research
Moira Daly
Virginia Neale

Design and layout
Heather Delfino
Margaret Hoogeveen

Printer
Worzalla Publishing Company
Stevens Point, Wisconsin

Photography acknowledgments
Cover shot: Zhao Meichang
Jim Bryant: p. 6(lower left), 8, 11(left), 15(top left), 17(main photo), 19(bottom), 27(top left and right), 31(top right);
Janet Byford: p. 5(bottom); John DeCosta: p. 12; Judy Davies: p. 7, 17(top left); Ken Ginn: p. 11(right),
14(top and bottom), 22, 24, 25(top and bottom); Alain LeGarsmeur/Masterfile: p. 5(top);
Ivanka Lupenec: Title page; Pat Morrow/First Light: p. 9, 19(top left), 29(top right);
Ruth Malloy: p. 13(top), 20, 23(top), 30(all three); Christine McClymont: p. 4(bottom), 13(bottom);
Gayle McDougall: p. 17(bottom right), 21(top), 29(top left); Courtesy of the Consulate General of the
People's Republic of China: p. 6(top and bottom right); Peter Reid: p. 17(top right), 31(top left and bottom right);
Larry Rossignol: p. 4(top), 6(top left), 10, 15(bottom), 18, 29(bottom); Courtesy of the Royal Ontario
Museum: p. 17(center right); Caroline Walker: p. 15(top right), 21(bottom), 23(bottom), 26(top and bottom), 27(bottom);
Zhao Meichang: p. 19(top right), 31(bottom left).

For my cousins
Paula and Christina

Cataloguing in Publication Data

Kalman, Bobbie, 1947-
  China, the people

(Lands, peoples, and cultures series)
Includes index.

ISBN 0-86505-208-5 (bound), ISBN 0-86505-288-3 (pbk.)
1. China - Social conditions - 1976   - Juvenile literature.
I. Kalman, Bobbie, 1947- II. Series.

HN733.5.C45 1989   j951   LC93-30924

Published by
Crabtree Publishing Company

350 Fifth Avenue	360 York Road, RR 4	73 Lime Walk
Suite 3308	Niagara-on-the-Lake	Headington
New York	Ontario, Canada	Oxford OX3 7AD
N.Y. 10118	L0S 1J0	United Kingdom

Contents

One billion strong

Over one billion people live in China. That's more than a thousand million! Throughout the past four thousand years the Chinese people have experienced many changes in their country. Their ancestors lived through times of war, famine, and flood, and several different systems of government. Out of this long and complicated history, the Chinese people have emerged with a rich culture and a strong spirit.

Recently, farming, industry, and trade have increased in China. Some Chinese people can now afford to own modern gadgets and dress in stylish clothes. They also enjoy hobbies and a variety of cultural activities, and thousands are traveling and getting to know their country.

Since China opened its doors to foreign visitors ten years ago, the rest of the world has also taken the opportunity to view the many wonders of this vast country and share in its rich traditions.

Hoping for a better future

Although many aspects of life in China seem better than ever before, the Chinese people have little say in the decisions made by their government. In June, 1989, thousands of students and other concerned citizens staged protests in Tienanmen Square. They wanted to bring about changes in the government. Hundreds were killed, and others were executed, but the cause continues to live in the hearts of millions. People all over China are still filled with hope for a better future.

Chinese people do not share only one background and lifestyle. China is a mixture of dozens of national groups whose beliefs and customs vary. One of China's challenges is to unite all its peoples even though they may live far apart and speak many different languages.

The Han clan

There are fifty-six national groups in China. All these groups have been living in China for a long, long time. The majority of the population is Han Chinese. The Han trace their ancestry and culture to the Han Dynasty, which ruled China for four hundred years during ancient times. The Han are bound together by common dialects of one language and a culture that is thousands of years old. They originally lived in the fertile eastern river basins, but over hundreds of years they have migrated all over China.

Non-Han groups

The fifty-five other national groups of China make up six percent of the present population. Six percent may seem like a small number, but it is still sixty million people!

The non-Han nationalities are called "minority groups" because they are greatly outnumbered by the Han Chinese and because each group has a unique culture. A long time ago these peoples settled within present-day China's boundaries, bringing new ways of life with them.

(clockwise from top left) A Bai woman carries her child in a backpack.

Bouyei women embroider their hand-woven clothes with flowers and symbols of long life.

On special occasions Miao women wear headdresses and large silver ornaments all over their clothes.

Bai headdresses have fringes. Single women wear long tassles; married women wear short ones.

(this page) An elderly Han Chinese man

Autonomous regions

China is divided into twenty-one provinces and five autonomous regions. Autonomous means independent. An autonomous region is a place where many people from one minority group live together. Although these areas are still considered to be part of the People's Republic of China, their inhabitants are free to follow their traditional ways of life. Dozens of smaller autonomous counties can also be found within areas where the Han Chinese live. These are home to several minority groups, such as the Miao, Bouyei, and Bai.

The five autonomous regions are Tibet, Xinjiang, Inner Mongolia, Ningxia, and Guangxi. Except for Guangxi, which is in China's mid-south, these regions are near the borders of China. Harsh climates and rugged landscapes have caused the people who live in these regions—the Uygurs, Kazaks, Kirgiz, Tibetans, Mongols, and Hui—to live in small, scattered communities.

Miao and Bouyei artisans

Many Miao counties are scattered throughout Guizhou province. The Miao live in unique hanging houses and wear delicately embroidered, homespun clothing. They are well known for their silversmithing techniques and finely crafted pottery. The Bouyei, like the Miao, also live in Guizhou province. They are famous for their blue-and-white carpets.

Compared to the rest of China, Tibet is an isolated area with few resources. Many Tibetans are poor and must struggle to survive.

The Bai

The Bai have lived in China's interior for over a thousand years. Today around one million Bai live in autonomous areas within Yunnan Province. Many work in marble quarries, as their ancestors did before them, lugging huge pieces of stone on their backs. Local Bai sculptors use some of the marble to create vases and other ornaments; the rest is shipped to far-off places to be used in the construction of buildings. When Bai villagers are constructing a building, they have a celebration after the roof beam has been raised. They throw coins baked in bread from the roof to ensure wealth. This celebration is part of Bai folk religion.

The Tibetans

The plateau of Tibet is located in southwest China, to the north of the Himalayas. The people living there, the Tibetans, depend on farming and animal herding for survival. They grow barley and keep large, shaggy, black animals called yaks, which supply them with meat and dairy products. Tibetans practice an ancient, unique religion known as Lama Buddhism. They are well known for their colorful clothing.

Life in the desert

The Uygurs, Kazaks, and Kirgiz are scattered across the northwest of China in the autonomous region of Xinjiang and throughout desert provinces such as Gansu. These groups continue to live as they have for centuries, depending on farming and herding for their livelihoods. Gravel covers the dry, hard ground of the Xinjiang region. The people who live there must endure extremely cold winters and scorching-hot summers. Sometimes the temperature climbs higher than 40°C; at other times it drops below -40°C. Sudden dust storms are common, and thick clouds of sand can completely blot out the sun. Because there is little soil, farming is difficult and limited. Crops can only be grown in the moist ground near an oasis. An oasis is an isolated area of land in the desert kept fertile by a series of underground springs. Turpan, an oasis north of the Taklimakan Desert, is the hottest and lowest spot in China. It is almost two hundred meters below sea level.

Homes of sun-baked clay

The Uygurs are farmers who live in adobe houses. Adobe is a type of brick made from sun-baked clay. Adobe homes have deep cellars that stay cool even when it is extremely hot outside. The Uygur diet consists mainly of lamb meat, rice, and fruit grown in the oases. Uygur women wear flowered skirts, dark stockings, and embroidered skull caps on their heads. The men also wear caps, along with knee-high boots and two-piece suits. The Uygurs follow the religion of Islam.

Living in yurts

Like the Uygurs, the Kazaks and Kirgiz follow the Islamic faith, but their lifestyles are much different. The Kazaks and Kirgiz are tent-dwelling nomads. Nomads are people who wander from place to place looking for food and land on which their animals can graze.

The Kazaks herd sheep and goats, and the Kirgiz herd yaks, goats, camel, sheep, and horses. The houses of the Kazaks and Kirgiz are dome-shaped tents called *yurts*. A *yurt* consists of many layers of felt laid over a portable wooden frame and tied down with ropes. When it is time to move, the entire structure can be folded up into a bundle and moved to another location.

The Mongols

The autonomous region of Inner Mongolia is located in the north. Six hundred years ago the Mongol people were the rulers of China. They came from Mongolia and started the Yuan Dynasty. After the Ming Dynasty took power, the Mongols settled in their current location—below the Mongolian border, next to the Gobi Desert. Like the Kazaks and Kirgiz, the Mongols have led nomadic lives for centuries. They, too, live in *yurts* and herd sheep and camels on horseback.

Around a hundred thousand Kirgiz inhabit China's far west. As nomads, Kirgiz carry only a few belongings, so their colorful, hand-woven wall hangings and rugs are used for many purposes.

喜   Family life   喜

The extended family has long been a traditional part of Chinese society. Extended families include family members such as grandparents, aunts, uncles, and cousins. In the past, Chinese homes were crowded because several generations lived together, and couples usually had many children. Villages were made up of several farming families that were often related to one another. Living in a Chinese village was like being at a big family reunion every day!

Enduring relationships

Even though Chinese couples have fewer children these days, and more people live in cities than ever before, the extended family is still a part of life in China. Most village families work together on the land or in factories. Elderly Chinese people usually live with their married children and grandchildren, especially

in rural areas. In cities it is common for three generations of a family to live together in one building because there are not enough homes for everyone.

Respect for elders

Older people have a special place in Chinese society. They are respected for their knowledge and experience. Their advice is sought and carefully considered in family decisions. Chinese grandmothers receive special treatment because they are considered to be the heads of households. People of the Chinese culture feel it is their duty to care for their parents when they are too old to care for themselves. Some cities provide "Homes of Respect for the Aged" for those who have no families to look after them.

In rural areas most people work with their children alongside them. In cities the state provides day care.

This newly married couple poses with two nephews.

Links with the past

Not only do the Chinese respect their elders, they also keep the memories of their ancestors alive. They believe that every person, living or dead, is a link in a long chain of people that stretches back to ancient times. Even though ancestors are dead, living relatives still feel that they influence daily life.

The changing family

The Chinese family has changed in many ways in the last hundred years. In the old days men and women did not choose their own marriage partners. Matchmakers brought them together. This practice is now illegal, although some marriages are still arranged in rural areas. Today most couples marry for love. To prevent large families, the government discourages people from marrying until they are in their mid-twenties.

Family jobs

In China, people of all ages have family responsibilities. If the grandparents have retired, they usually take care of their grand-children and do much of the shopping and cooking. These are very important functions because in many young Chinese families both parents work outside the home.

As well as having jobs, adults often sit on committees that help run their neighborhoods. Even the children contribute in some way. Village children may have to feed the chickens or mind their younger brothers or sisters. City children are expected to spend part of their time doing work for the community, such as cleaning classrooms or streets.

Separated families

In some families one of the marriage partners is required to take a government-assigned job in a faraway city. Couples do not like this enforced separation because it puts a lot of stress on family relationships.

11

喜　One-child families　喜

In the past, Chinese peasants had large families with lots of children. Children had many chores and also helped look after the farm animals. With several children, parents could be assured of being cared for in their old age. Even though there were many births every year, the population stayed about the same because just as many people died due to disease or starvation. Today, however, there are better sanitary conditions, medical services, and more food supplies. Fewer babies die, and people live longer than before. Every year the population of China grows by a whopping fourteen million people.

A poster encouraging one-child families

Special rewards

In order to control the growth of the population, the Chinese government has tried to convince couples to have only one child. The the one-child-family policy has been in effect since the 1970s. Couples that have only one child are given a bonus and do not have to wait long for a home. Visits to the doctor or hospital are paid for by the government. The child is placed at the top of the list for a spot in kindergarten or primary school. This is a great advantage because there is a shortage of teachers and classroom space in China.

Serious measures

Families that have more than one child are punished. For instance, the government withdraws the family allowance, gives that family fewer privileges, and makes it pay fines. The family that has a third child receives even harsher penalties. The child is put at the bottom of the list for a place in kindergarten, and the family must pay all its own medical expenses.

The Chinese government has made a remarkable effort to control its population growth, but the program has not turned out to be a complete success. Controlling population is a very difficult task. People do not like being told not to have children. Many people want families so badly that they are willing to pay the fines and suffer the other penalties for having more than one child.

City and country differences

One-child families are more common in the city than in the country. In the country a larger family can live more comfortably. Housing is not nearly as crowded, and children are still needed to help out with the farm work or family business. In 1988 the government decided that rural areas no longer had to follow the one-child-family policy. Minority groups are also allowed to have more than one child. Another change in the one-child-family law is that a city couple may have a second child if their first is a girl.

The children of one-child families enjoy special attention from their parents and privileges from the state.

Children

The ancient Chinese saying, "Children are as precious as jade," is truer today than ever before. With the one-child law in effect in China, parents and grandparents lavish all their love and affection on that one lucky child.

(circle) Rather than diapers, Chinese babies wear pants with slits. Like many Chinese grandparents, this grandmother lovingly looks after her granddaughter while the parents are at work.

(opposite, bottom) Chinese parents dress their children in colorful clothes.

(below) Several children can be taken for a walk in a pushcart. Sometimes day-care workers stroll along with a train of several pushcarts filled with smiling passengers.

In rural areas children have few toys so they play with anything available.

City children play at a day care while their parents work.

Chinese homes are built to suit the many landscapes and weather conditions found in China. To shelter them from the wind, some houses are built beside mountains. Others are built with deep cellars to keep them cool. Many houses in flood-risk areas stand on strong stilts. These designs suit the regions in which the homes are built, but they also reflect the cultures of the people who live in them.

Traditional houses

Older houses in China are one story high with white-washed walls. Their upswept roofs are made of overlapping dark-blue tiles. Support beams are often intricately carved with symbols that have been passed down through many centuries. Most houses consist of two large rooms, a kitchen, and a bathroom. Courtyards make up for these tight living quarters. Several houses face into one courtyard, where trickling fountains and moist plants help bring down the temperature during hot weather. Families and neighbors play games and eat outside in this pleasant atmosphere. Wooden gates close off the courtyard from the busy streets.

Difficult living conditions

Fresh running water is a luxury that people often take for granted. Many Chinese homes do not have indoor taps or flush toilets. Instead, the Chinese get their water from outdoor taps or neighborhood wells. It is still common to see people carrying home their daily supply of water in wooden buckets hanging from a bamboo pole across their shoulders. Electricity is precious in China. Today most city homes have electricity, but families only use it to light up one room. Central heating is even rarer. People must wear several layers of padded jackets and trousers if their houses are too cold.

Concrete communities

In recent years many new concrete apartment buildings have been constructed in China's cities. Groups of these five-story buildings are built close together to form apartment complexes complete with shops and schools. The individual apartments are quite small, so families usually have to share kitchens and bathrooms. These homes are provided by the government, so rents are low. People who make extra money under the government's new policies are now buying their own homes.

A cave called home

When you think of people living in caves, prehistoric cave dwellers probably come to mind. Yet millions of people in China's northern villages still live in cave-type dwellings that are both practical and comfortable. Easy to build, these homes stay naturally warm in winter and cool in summer. Some cave houses are dug out of hillsides. This permits their residents to use the flat land on the hilltops and in the valleys for farming. The most interesting cave homes are built below ground level. First a huge pit is dug into the soft, loose ground. Then houses are carved out of the sides of the pit, and the pit becomes a courtyard. Some cave homes have bricked-in fronts with glass windows.

Living on the water

Thousands of Chinese people live and work right on the water. They live on *sampans*, small cargo boats that cruise up and down China's main rivers. These people make their living by shipping goods to and from river ports. Most of them rarely have to come ashore. Instead of attending regular school, the children who live on *sampans* are taught by traveling tutors.

(large photo) In rocky areas hanging houses are built right onto cliffsides, just as this religious community is.

(center) Cavelike homes, factories, and schools, such as this one, are carved into hillsides.

(inset bottom) A Chinese family works and lives aboard their houseboat called a **sampan.**

(top left) The interior of a typical rural home

(top right) As cities grow, new apartment complexes are built to provide housing for new residents.

喜 Changes in city and country life 喜

China is changing rapidly as it races to become a modern industrialized nation. These changes are having tremendous effects on living conditions in both the city and country. Let's take a look at how the daily lives of the Chinese are affected by some of these changes.

Growing cities

About two hundred million people live in China's cities. The older cities have been highly populated for a long time, but now they are even more crowded. New cities are growing up along the rivers and wherever business is booming. Many people are moving to the cities hoping to find work.

Modern conveniences

People who live in China's cities enjoy a higher standard of living than those who live in villages. Cities are more modern, and a wider variety of goods is available. Although living conditions are cramped, most homes have electricity, gas stoves, and central heating. Many city people earn enough money to buy television sets and fashionable clothes. They also have more free time to pursue leisure activities such as hobbies. City living does have its problems, though. The large cities, especially Beijing, Shanghai, and Chongqing, are both crowded and polluted.

Village life

People who live in rural China work hard and lead busy and difficult lives. Families often do all the field work manually because farming equipment is both rare and expensive. All kinds of construction, from building roads to digging sewers, are completed by hand. Many villagers take on second jobs in factories when there is not enough work to do on their farms.

Lack of services

Remote villages have few of the advantages of modern society. Running water and electricity are rare. There is a great demand for these services, but it will take a long time before they are set up. Along with a lack of services, shortages of goods often occur in rural areas.

(left) People who live in cities such as Shanghai have access to public transportation, electricity, and better health care.

(opposite, top left) Although there are more shops and goods available today, many items are still in short supply.

(opposite, top right) A young girl operates a raft that is used to ferry villagers across the river.

(opposite) Villagers continue to wash their clothes by hand. Many rural areas are still without modern conveniences.

喜 Language and communication 喜

Chinese is an ancient language that is extremely difficult to master. A person learning it might think that two words sound identical but soon discovers that the words have different meanings depending on the tone in which they are spoken. *Fu*, for example, means both "happiness" and "bat," depending on the pitch of the speaker's voice.

A national voice

China is a huge country, and its people speak many different languages. The Chinese from one region often find it impossible to communicate with the Chinese from another region. In order to solve this problem, the Chinese government declared the Mandarin dialect, or *putonghua*, to be the national Chinese language. A massive campaign was launched thirty years ago to teach everyone this dialect. Adults who did not speak it took special evening classes. Now school children all over China are taught their lessons in Mandarin. National newscasts and television programs use this common language as well.

Learning to read and write Chinese is quite a task because it is such a difficult language. The government has made a special effort to teach everyone in China the Mandarin dialect.

Words as pictures

Chinese writing is different from the print on this page because it does not use a phonetic alphabet. Chinese characters, or pictographs, represent words instead of sounds. Each pictograph is like a picture that stands for an object or idea. There are more than fifty thousand symbols all together, but the average educated person recognizes only eight thousand. Imagine having to learn one thousand characters in order to read even a simple book!

The communication age

Since the late 1970s China has stressed the development of its communication systems. There are now over two thousand newspapers, four thousand magazines, two hundred radio stations, and three hundred television stations across the country. Television is quickly becoming the most important news source in the nation. Although many people own radios and television sets, telephones are still rare. China has also recently joined the computer revolution. Many businesses now rely on computers that use a simplified form of the Chinese language.

Computers are becoming more and more important in China, as in the rest of the world. This student is learning how to use a computer at his neighborhood "Cultural Palace," or community center.

Information walls

With over a billion people in China, spreading information is a huge and difficult task. The Chinese have a clever system for passing on important news. Information walls, called *dazibao*, are a common sight on streets and in factories. National newspapers, local announcements, and public education bulletins are tacked up on these walls. Anybody who has a comment to make can pin up his or her message for everyone to read.

In the days when emperors ruled China, very few people had the privilege of attending school. Only boys from the ruling class and a few brilliant peasants were given the opportunity to learn how to read and write. With the four treasures of study—ink, inkstones, paper, and brushes—these lucky students learned the teachings of the wise man Confucius.

Today every child goes to school. Starting at the age of seven, they stay in school for at least nine years. Many children also attend nursery school because both their parents work. After six years of primary school, students enter middle school for another three to six years. Those at the top of their classes go on to university to become professionals such as engineers, scientists, doctors, agricultural specialists, and teachers. Other schools are geared towards teaching various job skills.

A pinafored kindergarten class takes its morning walk.

Students go to school every day except on Sunday. In some schools Friday is excursion day and Saturday is spent in a park. Chinese children enjoy four weeks of summer holidays.

Jump, twist, and turn

In China the school day begins with ten minutes of exercise. Jumping, twisting, and turning makes everyone alert and ready to start classes at 8:30 a.m. At noon children take a two-hour lunch break and then go back to class until 4:30 p.m. In both rural and city schools children are responsible for cleaning their classrooms and school yards.

In the younger grades students spend a lot of time mastering the difficult brushstrokes of Chinese writing and the ancient skill of using the abacus. An abacus is a hand-operated computing device using beads as counters. It is like a calculator without batteries.

After-school fun

Most students do not go straight home after school. Instead, they go to one of the many recreation centers called "Children's Palaces." Here, children enjoy all sorts of activities including drawing, clay modeling, and dancing. Children who are especially good at one activity, such as gymnastics, receive extra training.

Rural education

For a long time there were hardly any schools in the villages. Children were needed to work on the farms, so few rural children attended classes at all. Rural schools are frequently small and poorly equipped even today. Sometimes the floors are made of earth, and several grades are taught together by one teacher.

In the past few years, many new schools have been built in small villages. A great effort is being made by the government to educate everyone, including the people in the most remote rural areas.

After school many city children go to their neighborhood Children's Palace and sing in the choir or participate in other activities such as dancing, art, or games.

These school children use colorful hoops as part of their daily morning exercises.

Making a living

Business is booming in China! Never before have the Chinese people known such prosperity. New businesses, such as street cafes, luxury hotels, and factories of all kinds have opened everywhere. Large billboards advertise modern appliances for sale at fancy, air-conditioned department stores. Ten years ago all these things were unheard of in China.

New policies

When the communist government first came into power in 1949, China was a poverty-stricken, war-torn land. The government took control of production and trade so everyone would have food, shelter, and a job. Then in 1979 China introduced two new plans—the open policy and the responsibility system. The open policy has enabled China to trade goods and exchange ideas with other countries for the first time since the nineteenth century. Millions of tourists have visited China in recent years. The money tourists spent contributed a great deal to the country's economy.

The responsibility system allows people to make extra money. Previously, people were paid the same wage no matter how hard they worked. As a result, the economy did not prosper. Now private citizens are starting up their own small businesses. With the extra

money people earn, they are able to buy factory-made goods such as bicycles, sewing machines, and electronic products.

Private farming

More than half of China's population still makes a living off the land. On some of the old farming communes, up to twenty thousand people worked together. Now these farms have been divided into smaller units so village communities and family work groups are in charge of their own production. Families manage private plots as well. Farmers hand over a portion of their crops to the government and sell the rest at the free markets. Free markets are markets that are not controlled by the government. At free markets, goods are sold at competitive prices instead of at prices set by the government.

Assigned jobs

Until recently most people were assigned jobs on farms or given work in factories. Although the pay was low, workers received many benefits, such as medical care, education, day care, and housing. Many people still work for state-run operations such as hydro-electric plants and steel factories.

New choices

Chinese workers have more choices than ever before. Now more people are allowed to choose their own careers instead of being assigned to positions when they finish school or training. Some people find a job on their own or with the help of a job-placement agency. Others open their own businesses. Universities are training more and more students to become doctors, engineers, teachers, and technology experts. These new opportunities have encouraged people to work harder for both themselves and their country.

(opposite) As China's business world expands, more and more executives can be seen in western-style business suits.

(right) This woman works in a government steel factory.

Many jobs in China still involve hard labor. Labor-saving machinery is rare. This man carries heavy loads of rocks up the staircase countless times in one day.

喜 Private businesses 喜

Since 1979 the Chinese government has been encouraging people to make money on their own. More than twenty-two million people have become involved in private businesses of one kind or another. Business owners range from pig farmers and flower sellers to restaurant owners and dentists. Many businesses start on the street. If the businesses do well and grow, street vendors sometimes rent stores and set up permanent shops.

A family-run fast-food stall

Cottage industries are businesses that are conducted in people's homes. Some early cottage industries have grown into huge factories that now employ many people. For example, a local artisan skilled in making ceramics may open a small shop operated from his or her home. The artist begins to train helpers as the business grows. Today there are thousands of privately owned factories that produce everything from fine leather shoes to bubble gum.

Private businesses often make more money than state-run operations, but their owners must also pay high taxes to the government. The pictures on these two pages show examples of just a few of the types of private businesses in China.

An outdoor dentist, opposite, showing his instruments and successfully pulled teeth

Father plays the **erhu**, *mother holds the speaker, and their child collects for their musical efforts.*

A family-operated noodle-making business

Artisans display their quilts at a free market.

Chinese people today have more free time than ever before, so they are participating in a wider range of leisure activities. City residents learn traditional arts and crafts at community centers or "Cultural Palaces." Country dwellers make their own fun. They play all kinds of games, such as cards and Chinese chess.

Outdoor fun

Because of crowded conditions, Chinese people live in small homes that do not have room for entertaining. As a result, they spend much of their free time outside. On summer evenings neighbors gather together in courtyards to play cards or chess. On Sundays many families visit historic sites such as the Great Wall or enjoy a rowboat ride in a park. Other favorite activities are gardening, shopping, and visiting with friends at local restaurants and outside cafes.

Parks and songbirds

Parks are used by people of all ages, but they are especially popular among the elderly. In China men retire at sixty and women at fifty. People are still very active at this age so they take up a number of hobbies. A favorite pastime of elderly men is training songbirds. These birds are kept in delicate bamboo cages. Their owners take them for walks to nearby parks where they hang their cages from trees. The birds relish the fresh air, and the owners enjoy admiring one another's pets.

Sports

Sports are popular with people of all ages. Ping pong, basketball, volleyball, swimming, gymnastics, and shadow boxing, are all favorites. Most Chinese participate in some kind of physical activity.

Ping pong

Ping pong may be considered the national sport of China because so many people play it. In winter it is played indoors; in summer it becomes an outdoor game. Outdoors, temporary tables are constructed by placing a table top on bricks or concrete blocks. Even the net is made out of a row of bricks! People play ping pong just about everywhere—in parks, courtyards, sports centers, and school yards.

Martial arts

Hundreds of different kinds of martial arts are performed in China. Many of these have taken centuries to develop. They were once used in combat against enemies. Today they are practiced by many people just to keep fit. Some martial arts are associated with religion, such as the *shao lin* boxing exercises. *Shao lin* was developed to help monks stay awake during long meditation sessions.

Tai ji quan

At dawn hundreds of people, including many elderly, dress in loose clothing and gather in parks or other open spaces to practice the graceful exercises of *tai ji quan*. *Tai ji quan* is a series of 128 body movements. The purpose of these movements is to keep the body in constant motion without losing balance or breaking concentration.

This gentle form of exercise developed from a religion called Daoism. Participants focus their energy and thoughts on moving smoothly and gracefully. Doing the postures is much harder than it looks! The exercises demand great muscle control. It is important to relax one's mind and control one's breathing. Most of the basic positions are named after animals and birds such as the eagle, bear, horse, cat, dog, snake, and leopard. Some of the movements are so beautiful that they are also used on stage in Chinese operas.

At dawn young people gather to practice the graceful movements of **tai ji quan.**

Boys enjoy board games on Sunday afternoons.

(right) An acrobat performs for an enthusiastic crowd.

喜 Linda's trip to China 喜

Millions of people have visited China. Linda was one of them. She was very excited when she heard she was going because many of her relatives live there. She would have a chance to visit Jook Yuen, the village of her grandparents. About seven hundred people live in Jook Yuen, which means Bamboo Garden. Everyone has the surname Lor, including Linda's grandfather.

On her trip Linda visited the village school that many of her cousins attend. The students did a special dance to welcome Linda. They gathered around so Linda's mother could take a picture. A boy showed her how to do calculations on an abacus.

On the way home from the school visit, Linda met a little girl carrying a baby on her back. Linda was amazed that, instead of playing with her friends, this little girl had to look after her baby brother most of the time.

On her last day Linda's uncle let Linda ride his water buffalo. It was fun! When Linda had to go home, she felt sad to leave her many relatives and new friends, but she knew she would always carry the happy memories of China with her.

喜 Your trip to China 喜

Perhaps after you have read all about China, you may be fascinated enough to see it for yourself. What are some of the places you would visit? How would you spend your time?

Would you watch a cormorant fisherman balance on his long, skinny raft as his birds dive for fish?

Would you go on a dragon ride in one of China's many parks?

Would you make a new friend and ask her to be your penpal?

You would most certainly want to visit the Great Wall. You could join thousands of Chinese tourists for a walk along this ancient, winding fortification. Did you know that the Great Wall is the only structure that can be seen from the moon?

Glossary

abacus - An ancient counting machine using beads on a wooden frame

ancestors - People from whom one is descended

autonomous - Free from outside control; independent

Buddhism - A religion founded on Buddha, an ancient religious leader from India

central heating - A heating system serving many rooms from one main source

civilization - A society with a well-established culture that has existed for a long period of time

communism - An economic system in which the country's resources are held in common by all the people and regulated by the government

commune - A community in which land is held in common, and where members live and work together

culture - The customs, beliefs, and arts of a group of people

Daoism - A religion based on the teachings of Lao Zi, an ancient Chinese philosopher

dazibao - The Chinese word for information walls where important news is posted

dialect - A way of speaking that differs from the standard language in some of its vocabulary, pronunciation, and sayings

extended family - A family unit including grandparents, aunts, uncles, and cousins living together

folk religion - The informal beliefs of the common people of an area

generation - People born at about the same time. Grandparents, parents, and children make up three generations.

industrialized - A term used to describe a society that produces manufactured goods in factories

Islam - A religion based on the teachings of Muhammed. Its followers are called Muslims.

Lama Buddhism - A religion that combines the teachings of Buddha and the Dalai Lama, the spiritual leader of Tibet

manual work - Work that is done by hand rather than by machine

martial art - A sport that uses the techniques of fighting and self-defense once part of battles and wars

minority - A small group that differs from the larger group of which it is a part

modern conveniences - Up-to-date goods and services that make life easier, such as electricity and running water

national group - People who share a common background and lifestyle

nomads - People who wander from place to place in search of food or land on which their animals can graze

oasis - An area of a desert that is kept fertile by underground springs

ornament - A small, brightly colored object used for decoration

pictograph - A picture used to represent a word

plateau - An area of flat land raised above the surrounding land

putonghua - The Mandarin dialect, now the national language of China

rural - Relating to the countryside

sampan - A small boat with one sail and a flat bottom, often used as a houseboat

sanitary conditions - Conditions that promote better health, such as cleanliness and proper sewage disposal

yurt - A portable dome-shaped tent made of many layers of felt laid over a wooden frame

Index

789 WP Printed in the U.S.A. 8765